SEX & LOVE &

Also by Bob Hicok

Elegy Owed

Words for Empty and Words for Full

This Clumsy Living

Insomnia Diary

Animal Soul

Plus Shipping

The Legend of Light

Bob Hicok

Sex & Love &

Copper Canyon Press
Port Townsend, Washington

ACKNOWLEDGEMENTS

Agni, American Poetry Review, Boulevard, Diode, Field, Frequencies, Georgia Review, Green Mountains Review, Kenyon Review, Narrative Magazine, The New Yorker, Pank, Poetry, The Pushcart Prize, Rattle, Southern Review

Printed in the United States of America

Cover art: Lorenzo Sala, *Hold Me Falling*, 2011. Photo printed on matte paper, size 50 cm x 70cm.

Copper Canyon Press is in residence at Fort Worden State Park in Port Townsend, Washington, under the auspices of Centrum. Centrum is a gathering place for artists and creative thinkers from around the world, students of all ages and backgrounds, and audiences seeking extraordinary cultural enrichment.

LIBRARY OF CONGRESS CATALOGING-IN-PUBLICATION DATA
Names: Hicok, Bob, 1960– author.
Title: Sex & love & / Bob Hicok.
Description: Port Townsend, Washington : Copper Canyon Press, [2016]
Identifiers: LCCN 2015040116 | ISBN 9781556594755 (paperback)
Subjects: | BISAC: POETRY / American / General.
Classification: LCC PS3558.I28 A6 2016 | DDC 811/.54 —dc23
LC record available at http://lccn.loc.gov/2015040116

Copper Canyon Press
Post Office Box 271
Port Townsend, Washington 98368

www.coppercanyonpress.org

For (though not always about) Eve

CONTENTS

SEX & LOVE &

Speechless

As shadows make the best groupies,
a cello's moan's more human
than any word or fire I have spoken.

Nothing sounds as much like my brain thinking
my heart sounds.

To be alive, they have to be warmed
between the thighs.

I bought one just to drag a bow across
the night, to make flesh the vibrations
of wanting.

To be alive, I have to be afraid of you, of time
dying.

The only sound that comes close — whales,
the plaintive ocean.

Where are we — so clearly
nearly nothing — going?

Love poem

The woman I love
braids her hair. She's Eve
and Eve means *breathe, to give life,*
my wife, from Eva by way
of the Hebrew *havah.* At dusk
I unlock her hair
from the curves it's learned.
Overnight it remembers
a simpler life. Come morning,
she misses weaving herself
into a basket. If we had only
this one ritual, I'd still
think the sky of my time
on this planet,
but there's more. We wake
and kiss and eat and kiss
and talk and kiss and walk
among cedars and grow lines
around our eyes and mouths
and kiss as our sex dries out
and falls down and touch
as if no one were ever evicted
by a snake from bliss, if you
(and I hardly) can believe it.

First light

The sky an insistence, little more.

Like when someone walks into a room,
sets a pitcher of cold water on a table
in the back, and leaves.

The pitcher sweats and so the room
has a bearing more like a woman
in bed, the window between her legs
open.

A sky like that.

Just barely touching itself.

A sigh of light against the eyes.

Before you even have to call it dawn.

Before she pulls your hand over
where her hand was
and sets it free.

L'eau de vie

The most liquid moments — waking
at one or two — rolling into her — mouth
first — cock second — neither of us
fully conscious or encumbered — liquid
in effect and feeling — with
the intelligence of rain — the
persistence of ocean — water
borrowing the shape of tongues, hands — the shadow
water of night — another dream
the body has — not one
speck of thought — & hesitation — what
is that?

After faster

We lie
laid — she
a cocoon of me
of me of her
in a reciprocal
wrap of arms —
the fraction
of fuck
that's friction
all over —
the faction
of affection
that's hump
all gone — leaving
a sleepy potion
of semen
and lubrication —
leaving love

Hot

The sexiest thing a woman has ever done
to or with or for me—while wearing the loose breeze
of a dress or standing inside its red zero on the floor—
while bending over and pulling her shorts down
on a racquetball court or to reach the water
shutoff valve behind the fridge—as Satie
whispers against our thighs or humming
her brain's native tune as we touch
the smudged glass protecting extinct beetles
in a museum—with her lips swaddling my tongue
or finger up my ass—is tell the truth—
which makes my wife the hottest woman
I've ever known—her mouth erotic every time
she speaks—she is an animal when it comes to sex
and love—comes to us—in that she doesn't primp
in front of the mirror of what she thinks I want
her to say or be—the only real flesh—only naked
that matters—how she looks at me

To join my religion, breathe

A fly keeps bashing into me.
Off the window.
The poems of Max Jacob.
Now it has come to rest on a piece of paper
beside the phrase "The Etymology of Jizz."
Jizz is not what you think it is.
Not this jizz.
This jizz is a word birders use
to describe the overall impression of a bird.
Sean Dooley says jizz is "the indefinable quality
of a particular species,
the 'vibe' it gives off."
The word is probably a corruption of *gist.*
I love the jizz of this fly.
I wish you could see it cleaning itself,
lithing hind legs up and around
and over its wings, legs that flow
more than bend—a river
has found me once again.
Every day,
I don't know how to use the word *miracle*
and how not.
Its use fits my tongue
like a sweat sock, its nonuse
fits my spirit like a corpse. My jizz
is my job and my job is to say,
Look, the void lost.
Where nothing might be, there is something.
A fly.
A whisper.
An us.

A proposal disguised as a story

Fortunately he'd covered the pen for his dogs
with wire mesh. Even then, coyotes
jumped on top at night and tore at the mesh
in an effort to get at the dogs,
so he'd come out and fire his shotgun
at the stars, which always survived.
After weeks of this, he dropped the barrel
and wounded a coyote in a leg, then finished it
with a blast to the head. The next day,
he dragged the carcass a little ways off
from the house. Vultures circled, landed,
and went to work on the bounty. Not long after,
he was sitting on a log at the end of his drive,
waiting for the whooping cranes
that visit the pond he can barely see
about an eighth of a mile away, when a woman
he often smiles at from his car walked by.
She stopped. He told her about the cranes
and she asked to join him. They talked
about the clouds, which were thin
white mustaches low on the horizon.
She commented that there really is
a cloud nine, cumulonimbus, which can live
as high as fourteen miles up, the highest
a cloud could rise. He looked up
and wondered how to measure fourteen miles
of blue. By the time he looked down,
a crane had landed. *I always think*
of conductor's batons, she said,
when I look at their legs. He tried

to think of something to say about music.
There was a piece (the "Pathétique"—
he'd only remember the name
months later, when they were in bed,
her back to him as she hummed a thing
that wasn't a tune but was not
not a tune, that pushed
into the space between formlessness
and structure) that had followed
or led him since he was nine, he heard it
every day and thought of it as part of him,
but to call it a limb seemed trite,
an aura inaccurate, a companion desperate,
so he nodded and imagined a crane
on its back leading an orchestra
with its weirdly hinged legs. This is when
she said she liked his smile and smiled
as she said so. Her ease opened him
to wanting absolution for the coyote.
He told her the story and she said,
without any prompting, that he did
what he had to and that it was horrible
we've left them no space to be what they are.
By now there were seven or eight or ten cranes.
An exact count was difficult from so far away,
but they worked together
on this knowledge that mattered only
because it allowed them to be a couple,
to lean their pointing arms into each other,
as if to make one body and one set of eyes,

until they agreed it was eight. Eight
ghostly birds. Settling on a number
seemed to pull the sun lower,
which changed the light, which closed
the space between them even more,
which allowed them to sit and say nothing
for long enough that, when they stood,
there was no question they were together.
They walked toward his house
as if they'd done this for years,
their long shadows playing a little
movie ahead of them, from the days
before movies, before light
could or needed to talk.

Love poem

For a time we licked toes & liked it
& neither of us asked the other to wash,
I realize now that we stopped
as abruptly as we began & never
feet, never ankles, never assholes,
a common theme among prostitutes: men
who want to beg to lick their unwashed
assholes clean, on or off a leash, never
that & I don't miss her toes
unless they're out of town & she
has joined them, then I miss her toes
as very much as I miss her & flesh, she
has more of it as she ages & I
have more of it as I age, more
to lick & not lick as we like,
it's as if there's a menu & she
is the menu & everything is allowed, minus
forever

The private life of flesh

She does not like her breasts. I've never known a woman
who likes her breasts. Never once or twice has a woman
known to me entered a room and referred to her breasts
as lovely or diplomatic or a temperate zone of abundant
economic opportunity. I like her not liking her breasts
and her breasts, she is modest and inadvertently hot
in the morning especially when I pull back the covers,
like bread dough with nipples and not advertently hot
if there is such a thing. It's like living with the mind-
body problem—she minds that she has a body and I know
that feeling of O my god I'm trapped in this falling-apart
house with legs, this proposition of bone and meat
that was assigned to me by a dresser of souls. One
of her breasts is of course bigger and smarter and leans
libertarian because symmetry is a taunt of some boring
paintings and I worry about cancer in every part
of her body to the point I listen for chewing sounds
at night when her breasts are dreaming. Is an ear
on a breast the opposite of a mouth against the sun
or the same thing as a child holding a blanket
over the eyes of the dark? Questions are better waterslides
than answers are grooms. I tell her, *You think your breasts
are weird, look at my testicles*, and she does look
at my testicles, and my testicles blush and turn away.

High fidelity

All of them, the shapes, I like all of them,
the shapes, the young, the unsagged this and that,
in skirts, all of them, the shapes, do follow
in pants, the shapes, unfallen, all of them,
and get, completely, the wanting, desire
has no sunset, the shapes, in blouses
and out of, that schoolgirl-uniform-pout,
that cheerleader-shedding-pom-poms, I get it,
all the panting, I do shape, the skirts in young,
the unsagged wanting, I sometimes picture
this one bent thus and that one looking up
with a smile against my cock, but how
after, talk or want to, even, if shapes, if we
are just shapes in a bed, one of us
old enough to be two or three of us
old enough to know all of them, the words,
matter, the talking, the shapes
of minds, of time, time is a shape
my wife and I share, our time, our shape,
our sexy memories of Paris and putting
our dog to sleep, all of them, the things
we've done and said in bed with us,
a big bed, and bigger every day

If I had merely said, She is good,
  would you have listened?

Days I followed her
footprints in the snow—
until sky warmed
and snow melted—days more
I slept where the trail
had ended—then new snow
brought her footprints back
to life—by my clock,
she was a snow ahead—I ran—
but when I ran, her footprints
ran too—her going
was truer and lighter
than mine—this happened
again and again—by now,
I am lifetimes behind—
at least two or three
of mine—and hers—her lives
are gold and many and all
have been lived beyond
my reach—this woman
who has never left my side

A vision

Taking a cue from pianos, I put felt
on my hammers, felt on my tongue,
and drove quieter nails and licked my wife
more like an étude — put felt

ahead of knew and grew a taller shadow
for the moon to chalk upon the river — I

have had the callused hands
of the Old Testament and the tender hands
of whispers upon my brain
this whole time, striking and stroking,
loving and clanging — if I had

to choose (I have to choose), we
would leave for summer right now
and never come back — the tall grass

brushing its soft and constant hello
against our hips, the day opening
like a green door in the wind
the wind can't close

Microcosm

My penis goes into my wife
a young boy and comes out an old man

Our porno

You give me head.
Your head.
What's inside it.
You tell me about being five and believing
when you hold your breath
you're invisible.
We hold our breaths.
No one can see us but each other.
Our breaths hold us up
from the inside out.
We have sex but entirely off camera.
Totally without a soundtrack.
Harming no actual horse.
Completely without a cum-shot.
The reviewers say, *Why no cum-shot?*
But being auteurs, we don't read reviews.
We eat peanut butter.
You tell me you believe animals have souls
of AM radio stations.
I put our cat to my ear
and listen to the truth.
You rearrange the putty of my face.
We grow old.
We apply moisturizer to hard-to-reach places.
The back.
The heart.
We move as slow as fog on crutches.
We die within minutes of each other.
There's the cum-shot —
two sacks of wrinkles, dead on a bed,
holding hands.

Aubade

Pussy sounds like porn or a twelve-year-old boy
trying to act fifteen. *Vagina* only feels right
if I wear a doctor's smock and make people wait
in a room with ancient magazines. Recombining them,
pussina seems a princess or former Soviet bloc country,
vagussy something vegans put on the table, when you,
to be polite, pretend you're crazy-concerned
about your health and have a full bowl.
I've tried addressing it as *Ma'am*
or *Your Secretiveness*, really it reminds me
of dawn, of dew when I go down on the lawn. Do you
do that? Get on your knees around 6 a.m.
and lick the shit out of the world?
All that gratitude for something soft
and moist. Birdsong a halo around your head
and tongue. The sun trying to hold
everything in its arms. I want to have sex
right now in this poem with the universe.
While physically that's ambitious, emotionally
I'm just getting started being a man.

Torn

The internet's all show, no actual cunnilingus
has transpired between us. This has been
smoke signals from eye to eye. And just
like the telegraph, the telephone
gave us a means to the ends of staying
ever closer to home, ever farther
from the ear we'd dot-dash
or whisper into, what a sad story
for flesh, marooned. First by the womb,
then the word traveled fast and free
of lips, now your hips can thrive
in my brain without entering my life,
I might as well be on the moon.
The evolution of communication's
to mythologize togetherness
as we drift entropically apart.
That's what the kids
call a thesis statement. But god
you're hot, and your crescendo
of breath so fully apes
the real deal, is it possible
we can be islanded and still come
to prefer absence to presence,
the digital to the palpable?
I fear the question answers itself
by nodding to the fact that I
can write a poem and you read it
with no hand having touched metal
or paper or words that don't dissolve

as soon as a switch is thrown.
Half of my soul says, get used to it.
The other million percent begs, don't.

The pregnancy of words

Eros scrabbles to rose and rage
to gear or *gare*, as in Gare du Nord,
where I trained into Paris from not
smoking pot in Master Mad, I'm sorry,
Amsterdam, with its canals
called *gracht*s and clocks
that bonged my homesick hours
at different times. Which is smite
for you violet types, a flower
that says "love it" if you listen. Me, I do
and don't feel it matters that evil thrives
in live, that we tinker and smash
everything down to bits and then
try to patch a path back home, it's our lotto
in life, to have no clue
what a natural disaster is
when that disaster is us. That's what I love
about the shrug, it says zilch
sans le mouth and becomes
more aerobic the more you admit
the less you know, you know? It's a jumble
out there, kids, with slips and slides
and elide's eally ool, depending
what's lopped off, as in light of hand
or slight of and, but I better stop
before you spot how sparse
this parsing is. Besides, what can I say
about language other than it's an anal egg
in need of one glorious u? Words
or sword—pick your *poisson*. Every time

I try to peak into speaking, the bag
of gab to learn what our noodles
are really up to, I get flummoxed
that the tools I use
are the stool I stand on
to see a way in or out. I can't even tell
if I'm more trapped or rapt,
if meaning's mean or play's
a dumbwaiter riding numbly
up and down. But have you noticed
read becomes dear
if you ignore the world
as you find it and find it in you
to swirl the word, in the way
solve and loves are the same
bones, different skeletons?

Aphrodite at eighty

To be young and feel
like a grenade — that you can walk
into a room and explode it
with your hips, your face —
all the men and women
and eunuchs turning to you
at once — a wind made — a storm born
of their lust — or whatever it is
we want of beauty — men
would actually tell me
I was a goddess — then offer me
their eyes — their staring
as if it were a marriage,
a house — now
I am old and whisper
past cocks without disturbing them —
finally the watcher, a shadow
among the harvest — do I
sound pleased — do you
believe me — more importantly —
do I?

No, you go first

I'll die before she does
probably. We fuck
and kiss extra so she can bank
affection and I've caulked
around both tubs and typed
an explanation for how to use
the generator when storms
knock the power out. I've also
marked up the window in my office
with a diagram of where clouds
turn pink in the morning
over the mountains, which she never sees
but will when I'm dead
and she can't sleep and comes up
to fill my ass-shape
in the chair I'm sitting in now.
Marked up with crayon
and left notes. A few
thousand in shoes and inside
her ears and on every leaf
for ten miles that I love her
and don't forget to turn
the heat down at night.
I'd like to be reincarnated
as her and for her
to be reincarnated as me
and go through the life
after this life
from the other side of the table
eating kale, which I don't eat,

and having a vagina, which I sort of
have wearing a penis disguise,
and looking at the world
through her brown eyes.
A dying man's allowed
one request and this
is mine — let me vanish first
& best. Love has made me
everything I am —
a coward.

The study of geometry pays off

It's surprising how much difference
an inch or two makes —

the change in angle
when she pulls her legs back
a little more —

to how deeply I disappear inside
her breath —

what is my heart then —

a zoo from which the gates
have been torn and melted
into spoons for all
the first graders to eat
as much ice cream as they want —

or a lion
who knows he's free now
but doesn't want to leave —

or a wind
at home in another wind —

holding its shoulders —

her shoulders —

all of life
in my whispering hands

Homeward bound

My penis was born a clitoris — nub
that reached out in me and grew deep
in Eve — only 10 percent of her clit
exists aboveground — think root —
think green — that she and I share
a sister history — we're even sensitive
in similar ways — ends of clit & cock —
which says so much about why we love —
ghost of same under different — of common ground
and cause — like our birth from stars —
from light and the death of light — and not
just us — man and woman, man and man,
woman and woman, whoever's within
whatever style of flesh you covet
or love, there's this origin we all
go back to — making sex the return
of the prodigal — every one of us —
when we come together — coming home

Guy talk

A cock is a bloodstick. Sex for a man
is sanguinary, though the cock
can't hold what belongs to the heart
for long. It borrows
to burrow. Eyes dilate, labia engorge,
but the cock is a changeling.
While nothing is sillier
than a flaccid cock rhymes with
placid sock—an erection
is a confession. It admits,
an extension of mind. Touching it,
my wife touches how I feel
about her, she loves that I want her
and I love that it speaks
my feelings so clearly, that it shouts
without changing the shape of the room.
What a weird vocabulary to carry
at the center of my body. There is also
shyness, a wish to enter, hide,
and wither. These qualities define
men—a need to be large and brief, bold
and inconsequential, to fill
by an action that erases. And while
I don't venerate my cock—
I've not named it, nor would I write it
a ballad—neither have I run from it
(though the image of my cock
chasing me through the Great Rift Valley
makes this day, at six thirty
in the morning, already a trophy).

The simplest way to put it is cock =
orgasm = peace. When I cum, I'm not here
or there or anywhere. Words like *place*
or *soul* or *breath* exist before and after,
have purchase and use, form and weight,
but during—everything in me
that wants language and everything
outside myself that will accept it,
that will wear words around their shadows
and inside their gravities—things
like *leaves* and *boats* and *clouds*—all of that
is gone and gone without wound. There's nothing
and it's a warm nothing, an embracing emptiness
that I'd never leave and wonder
whether I'm inside every second and don't know it.
Is sex how the sun feels all the time?

The nth aubade

Either the mourning dove in the shoe box
in the garage is strong enough
to fly or I'll be crushing
its skull when this poem is done—

punctures under the wings—

blood from its beak—

the cat I saved it from
rubbing against my legs the whole time,
purring of a changeless world—

with the same hammer
I just used to add trim to new windows
that are blind—

I was the backup dunce in school—

the one who'd fill in for stupid when stupid
was sick—

who thinks whispering to animals
makes up for war, makes up
for the appetite of hands—

who, when the teacher asked, *Does the universe
know you exist?* said *Yes, I think the sky
is all eyes*—

and was sent to the corner
the rest of his life —

where I've built a home
of wrong angles and doors
that refuse to close —

and lots —

and lots of bones

Ideas I've been kicking around

No offense, fellas, but statistically, hope
springs maternal — we're aces at sperm
and murder — wired to fuck
and fuck things up — that's the clan of men —
but any one man — your pops or mine
or me or you — might tool around
channeling lambs — more soft
than jagged — so I gotta ask, what's
the supposed-to here? — are men
supposed to be bombs
to women's wombs — the dick-storm
that scatters what other winds gather —
the chaos that stirs the genetic soup —
I know that theory's out there
explaining football, bullfighting, spitting —
justifying stabbing and raping
and every trend in bloodletting —
but poems suck at big notions
removed from actual heads — so I'll reel this in —
make it small and confessional — I worry
slash-and-burn's the real artistry of men —
that I'm here less to kiss
than to make shit go boom — and that
the only sensible thing to say to my wife
is *Love you, hon — now save yourself — run*

Churn

Standing among shadow starlings
chased across the parking lot
by a hawk, we looked up
into the murmuration as it dervished
into a black sail that pinched
into an hourglass that amoebaed
into an arrow that softened
into a breath the sky was taking

It's as if emotion left our bodies
to be acrobatic and let us watch
how lovely we'd like the currents
inside ourselves to be,
is how this poem is deciding I felt
beside Home Depot, as the hawk
gave up and the starlings
settled upon the various
tall everythings they could,
overhead wires and branches
and two in a reclusive mood
on a Stop sign

Those two are us at a party, she said
as we entered to unbeautifully
buy nails, buy caulking
to keep wind in its place,
and returned to starlings
erased from every surface,
though they haven't left me—

they are how I try to touch her,
chased as I am by my own hawk
across the hours, falling
into the shape I hold
as it erases me, flying second
by second from elation to doubt, touch her
shadow-soft yet churning with the swift
and graceful chaos of the mortal wing,
so my name would be the only she could whisper
if asked by God or the hush we'll slip into at the end,
who was your favorite storm, your adored calamity,
who kissed you most like hunger?

Wedding vows

As much as I'd like to make
an intellectual case for monogamy, I can't
claim more than it suits me to hold hands
with one woman at a time, this keeps
one hand free to wave at fog or play
the piano as we walk, we have a piano
instead of a dog, and all that stuff
I need to tell one woman, to tell two
would be boring and twice as embarrassing
as life, there's also the dilution of joy,
for to cheat on saving the possum baby
by also saving the possum baby
with another woman, would ruin
our new family, the one of us
with full-moon areolae and the one
with wrinkly cock and the one
who lives in a box, but really
the difficulty of being fused
to more than one woman
is spatial as much as romantic, where
would three heads join, seriously,
in a bed that slumps already
so much in the middle, we sleep
in a valley and fuck in a valley
and that's it for the valley,
everything else we do together
takes place on even, on solid ground

No two snowflakes alike

She wanted me
to spank her. I had never
spanked, only been
as a child and not
sexually, one
hopes. Do I leave
underwear where
it is or strike
both high
and low were
questions and
hard, how
hard? That one
she answered, the rest
I had to work out
over a period of
I'm still not sure
moments or why
she came so
fiercely, but that's
the orgasm
all orgasms
are measured against
and found
different, each
from each
and even
from themselves.

Standard of measurement

Take the softest blanket (I forgot my childhood
blanket and Mr. Kopeckie up the street slandered it
as a rag while changing oil) or the softest rain (the one
in front of me is acting the part of a whisper
at the bottom of a canyon) or the most read psalm
on the softest page of the bible (23rd) nothing
is softer than she is soft where she is softest (yes
I'm thinking of her eyes how softly she closes them
when I touch the second-softest part of her) though
privacy is softer still (what she feels & I) & sex
the softest confession of these interiors (how soft
I wonder with my brain is the brain) sex a proxy
(a fever proxy) the closest we can come to touching
where touch resides

Working out

A man once asked that I hold him

down doing lat pulls—keep him

from flying in the gym—put my hands

on his shoulders and lean

as he pulled against the weight

of the machine—I did

feel for him what I feel

for women

briefly—muscle,

to the closed eyes

of my hands, the same parade

of flesh—the draw of heat

inward—and knew

for a flash I could let

go of everything

if different

were not so

Constitutional

Your grandmother — and not just her dementia
but anticipating your mother's, your own — walking
is who we talk about — away from town —
in the hospital again today you miss — up hills
until we can look back at the new theater
the university spent millions to have difficulty
filling — far away and far away — a drive of hours
and her thinking you are her daughter —
asking for her husband but meaning his ashes
to hold — that part is sane — is genius heart —
walking hand in hand — most intimate touch —
most unruly August sun — the space between your eyebrows
a thorn of fear — every night a walk and every night
her erasure and the vanishings to come — a walk soon
in the dark — the last flowers and the last of her love
of flowers — her final sensible words — where
will her words go when she is only face — talking
our way through walking — walking our way to hush —
until walking forgets for the body the mind
a while — that you will be — I will be — husked.

Well yes, maybe

Her grandmother is dying
to die but the nurses aren't letting her
and sound in their squeaky shoes like basketball
has no mercy. My wife and I step outside
and breathe as deep as stars
are far away, take the Milky Way
into our lungs near the banished smokers
and the crickets, who want so badly
to be noticed by each other it's as if
they're in high school, and I hold her
and turn slowly to the left, then come back
the other way until we're completely
different people, in that time
has passed and neither of us
has taken our heart out and placed it
in the crook of a tree. I love her face
not crying and crying exactly
like a wadded-up piece of paper,
a stepped-on orchid after the dance,
and tell myself that if we can act
the part of people who belong somewhere
for just forty more years, everything
will be fine. The food. The fear.
The wine. Everything. Fine.

A family matter

Of course, when my mother asked
that I give my wife a kiss for her, I did so,
telling my wife, *I am my mother, kissing you.*

My wife's mother, it turns out, had asked the same,
so of course she told me, *I am my mother,*
kissing you back.

When we informed our mothers later
that they had kissed as lesbians
through heterosexual proxy
beside our cat's sense that something
like a mouse or with the potential
to be a mouse would eventually move
through the spot she was staring at,
where nothing was or had ever been, as far
as the record shows, my mother asked, *Was tongue*
involved?

My wife and I consulted the log
but there was no entry. We shrugged
at our mothers and went about our lives,
though now with an awareness
there are gaps we'll never fill
that may or may not have tongues in them,
though given a vote, I say, *Yes, tongues, red*
like our mouths are where flames go
to understand what it feels like to us
to be alone.

I pause for menopause

A woodpecker
with a bit of red
in its array
has been haunting
the feeder.

The blood of it
comes and goes
on the clear ocean.

My wife's period
is gone.

I didn't get
to say good-bye.

Now all
the children
we didn't have
are older and never
call.

One plus one is three

The deer didn't move — on our walk — little deer
where the path turns toward the road — I spoke to it —
said *My you're pretty* — said *We should do this again* —
in my best holding-a-baby-in-my-arms voice — and slid by —
and felt as I did when my pants came back
from the dry cleaner's with wild roses in the pockets —
I called — the woman who picked up was crying —
I cried a hard rain in solidarity — the roses
were hers — *I wanted someone else to see*
what the Earth had done — not three feet away —
an arm — a rifle between me and the cereal-bowl
eyes of the deer — I wore the rose pants
for weeks without telling anyone they were standing
beside a garden — and didn't look back — afraid
I'd break something — afraid the deer would turn
into Eurydice and melt away and ruin this life — the one
I keep bumping into — the one that has river stones
in its mouth — until the roses had forgotten
they were roses — even when I told them
the story of dirt — of sun — of the reaching
they had embodied — all their efforts to hold up
the air — eyes full of grain and fear
withstood — showing me how astonishment is done

Almost full

Moonlight on her breasts: I'm being cuckolded
and made to watch.

One thought is to touch her shoulder
with my fingertip.

If she wakes, we'll make love.

If she keeps sleeping, I'll rise and write a poem
in which she wakes to that snowflake of urgency.

Moonlight is sunlight in a borrowed dress.

A wedding dress.

A dress a mother gives a daughter to give a daughter
to give a man.

All those ruffles, all that searching for the body

inside the dress, for the blood inside the light.

If I touch her, where I touch her, moonlight
will stop touching her.

I don't think I can.

They look so happy together, her briefness beyond language
wearing a radiance that will never come again,
that's so shy, I'm afraid if I move, it will bound away

like a deer.
So I watch, a voyeur of beauty, watch and feel
I'm remembering a song I've never heard,
which I know how strangers would sing
in a country I'll never get to—

as hard as I run or row, as long as I swim or crawl—

sing of love, of love that is wanting to have
the wanting to hold, songs that make you cry
while you sing them, songs you love for breaking you—

those songs, this moon, these breasts, this woman—

the only necessary list.

Friends

Sunny.
The kind of day no one
should tell you
they have cancer
she told me *These*
have to go and pointed
at her breasts.
She has no one
and asked me
to touch them
good-bye. Twenty
years I had had
no nipple except
my wife's in hand
or mouth. I said *No*
and left and came back
and said *Yes* and left
and came back
and said *No*
and stayed. *At least*
look, she asked. I
at least listened
to her shirt fall
with something
of a breath sound
or wind waking up
the shadow of a tree.

Paris

Le Champ de Mars.

Dark surrounding your body
with its dress
as your dress falls.

Warm blood
filling your nipple
in my mouth.

As close as I'll get
to biting your heart.

Shhhh

Three times we never talked once
about up her ass — even shitting
spunk out, there was no said
said — though we toileted
and shopped and everythinged
together — and gabbed ceaselessly
A to Z — not about that —
as if to pretend the minds
we had in bed weren't ours
but dreams wearing our flesh
for their own ends — oh,
and her miscarriage in the crapper
at the bar — when she didn't know
she was pregnant and we
drove separate & she
bloody home — we never
even mumbled round the edges
of that — or pinned words
to the silence itself,
let alone the panther
eating a dead rabbit
inside it — & went lickety
from close to far — other places
I never should have gone
or got to go — my folks' safe
to steal their dough —
into the locked room
where she slept/wept
when the babying stopped
alone — leaving it

for me to be decent in some
other life—whole in some
unwritable poem

When things that never happen happen

She saw a fox. I was driving
and saw a road. As soon as I could,
I pulled over and kissed her eyes.
She closed them when I did. I told her
Keep them open. She tried, but her reflex
was to close her eyes and see the fox again.
I have a theory of mystery, I just don't know
what it is. The next time we made love,
I looked for the fox looking down at me.
All I saw was my wife, the wildest dream
to ever take me under its wing.

Yom Kippur

I offer thanks as a complement
to atonement —

if she's alive, the woman who'll never read this
is near sixty — I was helping my brother
paint her father's house — she had just peed —
gone in from tanning herself in the backyard —
white bikini — tall, as if early on, the world
had asked for more of her — I went in to pee after —
sat down on her warmth — I was nine and she touched me
through the proxy of the toilet seat — nothing
wet happened — this is not a sticky poem —
only my skin became a flock of starlings
taking off — a murmuration — I left that bathroom
aware of a body inside my body — she was back
on the chaise — I could tell you about her ass
or breasts — we could go that way —
but you'll never see her — her beauty
is a privacy — and I'll never see her
as I'd like to — in her diminishment, her sag,
but still brilliant at the core — and tell her
about getting on my knees and sniffing
where she'd sat — molecules of her
entering my life — carried all these years
through fog and rain — to Paris and Sarajevo —
think of all the people buried alive
inside you — that language allows us
to put it that way — or enshrined, I should say,
given how I feel today — fortunate —

and ready now to apologize
for every wrong thing I've done

Getting by

I love the idea of climbing a ladder
while carrying another ladder. Of climbing that ladder
carrying a tree. Of climbing the tree
to get closer to where rain
doesn't fall, to touch the asceticism
of the sky, the hem of drought.
As when the woman I love said
I don't love you anymore and I decided
to love her for not loving me.
Within a year, she loved me again
for loving her negations. In the same way,
I love the rain for killing itself
before it reaches the grass, I love the grass
for turning brown, I love brown
for being the color of my thirst, I love my thirst
for its willingness to kill me. But this is all
an idea, a man on a tree on a ladder
on a ladder on a planet in a solar system
in a poem that is fighting for its life,
like the city I see when I close my eyes,
or the night of my closed eyes
that falls upon the city, or the people
in the city who look up
and want moonlight, even a quarter moon,
even the word *moon* on a string will do.

Why we must support PBS

"I didn't think of it as killing them," the executioner
from the late eighteenth century said to Charlie Rose,
still wearing a hood, his ax resting on the wood table
I've assumed is oak. "I don't know how to put this:
it's as if I loved them in the moment I swung, loved them
and wanted to offer them peace." Charlie Rose was smiling,
excited. Even more than usual, the joy of an otter
seemed to be swimming through the long river of his body
when he put a hand on the man's memoir and said,
"But then something happened that made you question
your entire existence up to that point." It was hard
to see the man all in black on Charlie Rose's black set,
as if midnight were speaking, saying, "Yes. One day
I looked down and there was the son I'd never had
staring up at me from the block, I could tell
by his eyes, this was my boy, this was my life
flowing out, reaching beyond the sadness of its borders."
"You knew this," Charlie Rose said. "I knew this,"
the executioner replied. "Even though you'd never been
with a woman." "Never. I was all about career." "You knew
because the eyes tell us something." "Because the eyes
tell us everything." "And you couldn't go on." "No.
I couldn't go on." They changed gears then and honestly
I drifted off, half dreamed I'd arranged a tropical-
themed party on a roof without testing how much dancing
and vodka the roof could hold, people were falling
but still laughing, falling but still believing
there was a reason to put umbrellas in their drinks,
that otherwise their drunkenness would be rained on,
rained out, when I heard the executioner say, "We

were running and running. Finally we made it to the border
and I put my arms around my son and told him, you have a future
but no pony. Get a pony." Charlie Rose smiled
like he was smiling for the otter, for whatever is lithe
and liquid in our spirits, and repeated, "Get a pony."
"That's the last time I saw him," the executioner said.
"And that's why you've refused to die." "Yes."
"To keep that moment alive." "Yes." "And you believe eternity
is an act of will." "Yes," Mr. Midnight said. "Will.
Will and love. Love and fury."

Artistry

The little boy reaches in, grabs a piece of his shit
and takes it to his father,

it's orange, it's never been orange before,

in the garage, his father's in the garage,

a hammer in his right hand and his right hand
behind his right ear,

the hammer behind his right ear about to come down,

about to smash a board he's furious at,

it refuses to be beautiful, this board, this board
has split on one end, this board has no thought
for the cabinet he's trying to make for the urns,
the urn of his wife and the urn of his mother,

when the sound, the sound of *Daddy*, the sound of *Daddy*
saves the unbeautiful board,

the father turns and there he is, his son, his son
holding a piece of orange shit, a shit better
than any shit the father has ever created, ever been
the author of,

he sets the hammer down, the father, the father
sets the hammer down and the board lives,
the father sets the hammer down and says, *Wow*

with a hand on the boy's shoulder, his left hand
on the boy's left shoulder,

both of them looking at the shit, the orange shit,

He didn't get mad, the boy is saying to his wife,
the man is saying to his wife,

My father, he didn't get mad, the man is saying
of when he was a boy, a boy holding a piece of orange shit,

He said wow, the man is saying to his wife,
He said good for you, the man is saying to his wife
of when he was a boy, a boy with his father's hand
on his shoulder,

a nurse coming in, touching a machine, smiling at them,
a nurse wearing a top that wants to be a garden, a garden
touching a machine listening to the father, a machine
with its ear to the father's chest,

the curtains open,

night resting its forehead against the glass

In memoriam

A path of thirst
between the house and well.

I carry moonlight
in a bucket
for her to drink and wash,
taste moonlight
on her face and crotch.

Holes in the roof
for stars to get in.

No one comes here,
not even us.

Every year, I move his grave
a foot closer to the sea.

But I'm a coward.

I take the easy way.

I move the sea.

Mirror mirror

I am bald, sag-assed
& slouch-gutted, bald
& nearly enough hair
on my shoulders
to comb, bald
& temperamentally
erect, the uncertainty
principle alive
in my cock,

yet she looks at me
the same
as she's looked at me
since the first time
she looked at me
on William Street,
I believe, the secrets
to old age: love
and destruction
of every photo
of yourself
when you were young

Friendship (half hitch)

First time I couldn't
get it up, I said
it's like pushing a rope—
my wife said that's a pretty
short rope—I pulled hard
and tried to tie it
into a knot—we laughed
and went to breakfast
at the place we like
that's famous for miles
for being a lot better
at lunch

Secrets

I'm afraid
I'll never look
like the sun.
That all my seasons
are winters now.
That sleep has become
more erotic than sex.
That my cock
has stopped.
That my cock's
a stopped clock.
That I don't mind.

The novel of a minute

Plaster under my right thumbnail — "New York, New York"
stuck in my head from watching a Sinatra bio —
I'd just admitted to myself that sexual desire
had become less a wave that overtook me,
more a wave I had to chase — a cardinal
in the maple, living-red against the fresh-green
of April 11 — taxes on the table in large
white envelopes I didn't want to open —
Bishop poems under them and student poems
under her love of Nova Scotia — a dull knife
to the right I'd run between two fingers
harder and harder, wondering whether
it would cut — not just sexual desire
but the desire to move — to push against air
or walk up to a doorbell and ask the question,
Am I wanted? — a red fox the day before
had crossed the yard and stopped
where there's a gate but no fence, the gate
still trying to tell the story of transition —
stood looking and being looked at then
and looked at again in my thoughts
when I noticed what had to be her hairs
on the table — our dead cat — the cat we'd killed
a week before — four of them next to the salt —
picked one up and swallowed it and decided
not to lie — not to call my father and wish him
Happy Birthday — not to be in favor of time
passing ever again — tried the knife once more —
harder — finally a little bit of blood —
sucked on it — realized the only other blood

I'd tasted was a woman's — we didn't know
she was bleeding until there was blood
on my tongue — of the child — didn't know —
I wonder if a bed has ever held someone's shape
years before they get in — wanted
like that — I want to be wanted like that —
as a premonition — as whatever is the flip side
of a ghost — only because that's how I want you —
how I need to believe I want you — any — all
of the beings I love

Bird on a wire

I find her last posted smile
on a server that preserves her—
has no mind for the distance
between was and is—or obit—
end date—I visit to pretend
she's just back from digging wells
in Eritrea—or yesterday
confessed to hating quiche—both
eating and saying it—it's
the new mourning—electric tomb
more weighty than any grave,
though weightless, except the next-
to-nothing light weighs—
the new haunting—all I have to do
is miss a lot and drink a little
too late for sane
to find myself clicking
on every instance of her name—
woman I tried *lover* with,
and when we laughed at that,
discovered *friend*—and there she always
is, glowing—digital people
ghostly shine—they're charged—
pixelated—which takes me
to pixie—to fairy—to sprite—
to spry—to alive and too
alive, it feels almost
like killing her all over
and being told a brand-new
first time every time

the same fresh news
of gone — which is the point, I guess —
to abrade — degrade — to rub down
and out by repetition
the supposition that she's merely
a call or ride away — the juice
our bodies have that can't
be given back is almost
on-screen, the pulse
that whispered through her — and the hum
of my computer — a fan I hear
as dear as breath

Intro to biology

Sperm live three days
before replacement thrashers
arrive — red blood cells, four months,
tops — there are trillions
of cells and trillions of ghosts
of cells in our bodies, we are hauntings
of ourselves — the brain, only the brain
is honestly mortal — neurons
live and die once — not if but when
I forget the way you sleep, as if a soft rain
were falling inside your closed eyes — you won't
grow back in me — the brain,
only this brain touches you with words
softer than hands —
softer than the shadows the years gather
in our mouths

Closing the circle

My mother's eighty-two, I'm fifty-three,
I should probably breast-feed one last time
before there's nothing of either of us left
to look down a well or leave a camera
with the shutter open beside a road
at night for a photo that gathers
the smears of taillights — even though
she's dry — dry as tax law
unless you write tax law — dry as Clausewitz
unless you like war — and have her take me
over her shoulder and slap my back
until I burp — all one hundred
and seventy pounds — my mother singing
the whole time — *Take these broken wings*
and learn to fly — but how to ask — in a letter —
through an ambassador — and if she says no —
how to sit together and not feel
the awkwardness of the image — my grown mouth
on her dying nipple — the desire to be civil
versus the desire to go home — and what kind
of parasite was I? — a biter? — did I prefer
the left to the right? — and was there something
in her milk that loved fog, for I love fog —
that loved silence, for I can't get over
how impossible silence is — real silence —
for everywhere I go, there's my breath
speaking — there's my mother's breath
in my breath, speaking back

Hey sailor

She was always the one
tied, I could not
take jail or anything like
rope on my wrists, more
ceremoniously than
scrupulously, we never
talked about it when
the tying was tied
or untied or even
talked about the not
talking about
the tying, I could always
tie a tie, like
I was born to the Windsor
knot, if not
to the manor born, sheep-
shank reminds me
of shipshape and
her, still

Varieties of cool

A friend had a friend who winked us past rope lines,
we were enskied for one night in hipness

it was boring

the champagne tasted no better than wonderful

the music was the same lobotomy of thump
that had been playing for years as dissent
from our Puritan roots

then we freed ourselves in a cab, something yellow
that wasn't a flower but wanted to be, sang
"Homeward Bound" passably to be happy about melancholy
and teach the driver from Sri Lanka a thing or two
about the American wistfulness for home
all the way to the Brooklyn Bridge
and walked across the night and water
that I got down on my belly and said hello to
through the wooden slats

in Brooklyn Heights we ate grapes and waved
at all the effort by the various Carnegies
and Seagrams to live forever, my friend had a cough
that became an acronym, I sat beside his missing
a man with my missing a woman in front of homes
we knew from movies but appeared less famous
than cozy at four in the morning as we tried
to decide which house wanted to adopt us

I couldn't get over the grapes

he said, *That's New York, you can get anything*
as long as it's not what you really need

he didn't say that

I'm confusing him with Mick Jagger and this poem
with a novel, he said something and I did
back and forth, it was quiet and that's how
conversation works, the grapes were good
and the night air had no idea how bad
his cough would get, I am grateful
that, on balance, the absence of stars
in Manhattan is offset by the number of lights
there's no reason to leave on but people do

A picture is worth eight hundred and eighty-seven words

Her name was Alison. Alison or Beatrice. Beatrice
or Hiacinth. Like the flower but not spelled
like the flower. I'm not one of those guys
who forgets women's names. I'm one of those guys
who's distracted, in this particular constellation
of memory, by having taken a picture of my penis
long ago that did not include my penis. Things
were going well with Alison or Beatrice or Hiacinth,
so well we knew we'd make love soon, or to wax
pronounly, we knew we were going to do it. But Alison
or Beatrice or Hiacinth was very honest and very smart
and very shy and very hurt at least once, for she had
the idea that we each take a picture of our naked selves
and share these photographic confessions. That way,
if one of us didn't like what we saw, we could demure
without rejecting actual flesh, actual maybe sagging
or strangely asymmetrical or gothically tattooed flesh,
in the moment of its unveiling, that phase of a relationship
that should be accompanied by the phrase, *Ta-Da*. I loved
the idea, the overwhelming sense of photo-realism
it would add to my life, but when I stripped,
brought the camera to eye and aimed it at the mirror,
I laughed, laughed and thought, *Johnson, wang, schlong,*
puddle rudder, meatcycle, and noticed once more
that the penis, especially the flaccid penis, appears
to be what God was working on when the phone rang.
So I tucked it between my legs and snapped away.
In tucking it away I was tucking away
the absurdity of language and the organ's
significant lack of utility in its casual state

of existence. It was a whim, honestly, not an admission
of a secret wardrobe or dimensional concerns,
and knowing Alison or Beatrice or Hiacinth
as I thought I did, I felt she'd find it cute, endearing
even. That one day, we'd tell our oldest child,
when we were secretly stoned, just to make her blush,
to make him vomit in his brain. But. After the date
when we exchanged envelopes, I never heard from Alison
OR Beatrice OR Hiacinth, whose picture, by the way,
revealed not only a beautiful woman, but also a fine sense
of composition, due largely to the Van Gogh print
behind her left shoulder that suggested she was,
among other things, a starry night. Minutes to hours
to days to weeks, time did what it does that makes us
compare it to sand and water and really old people
in orthopedic shoes. When I couldn't take it
anymore, couldn't abide that she ignored my calls
and wouldn't ring me up, and accepted
that I didn't want to be a stalker, as lovely
as the lifestyle sounds, I did what anyone would do
who once attempted to unfreeze a gas cap with a lighter.
I bought a tube of lipstick—Cherries Jubilee, I think,
because of course a lipstick called Cherries Jubilee
would be cheap and noticeable—and wrote
on her windshield, I HAVE A PENIS. If you're thinking,
a note would have done, a letter, a message
on her answering machine, some skywriting even
would have been better, I have only this to say:
you obviously have a frontal lobe, whereas I
would need to drill down for proof before I'd commit

to having such a gray possession as that. So I'd written
in large letters what I never thought I'd have reason
to write, when this woman, this older woman in sensible
everything—sensible coat and shoes and hat and skin,
I found her skin eminently sensible in how it held
the parts of her that were supposed to be inside
inside—stopped and gave a little tug on her dog,
her dachshund I want to say, probably
because I had a dachshund as a child, Snippy
the *miniature* dachshund, which even at ten
seemed redundant, for I saw no especially large dachshunds,
no Godzilla dachshunds I needed to worry about
distinguishing from the lesser dachshunds, she stopped
and gave a tug on her dog and read what I'd written
in my frankly impressive block letters, I was and remain
quite legible, whether confessing I have a penis
or writing on the whiteboard on the fridge, EGGS,
PEACE OF MIND, so my wife and I won't forget
what we want from life, she was there and leaning
toward the windshield, the dog leaning
the way dogs do when people stop, as if they know
it's a mistake for living organisms to stop, ever,
she leaned and looked at the windshield, at me,
at the windshield, at me, and whispered
very softly, as if her lips were tiptoeing,
as if her voice were a match in a room of gasoline,
So do I. And smiled. The best smile I'd ever seen.
A smile that made me think she'd waited her whole life
to admit this to someone on the street, someone
with obviously a few things to work on. That became

the Cheshire smile, the smile that hangs in the air, that follows
and gives me the feeling I can yet be who I am.
And her name was Alison. Alison. Alison. Like the song.
The beautiful song I'm singing as I type this,
singing in my head, where I'm a wonderful singer,
as are we all.

She

When they take my life apart,
on the back of one board
of everything I've built,
they'll find "I love Eve"
written in whatever pencil
I had in my mouth
as I hammered and sawed — even

on the inside of my skull —

along with ochered handprints
and a few scratches
to get out — her name —
two letters, one word —
my answer to the question,
Does light arrive
or darkness leave?

The clock of the long now

There will come a time when stars
have sailed beyond the strength
of light to reach this valley, when the night
will no longer be interested in us.
I open the window. The cool air
against my forehead reminds me
the house is adrift. It seems moored,
as my head seems shouldered,
but my head is cut off and held
in my hand like a lantern. This doesn't
make me sad. Or makes me sad
in a way that becomes a happiness.
Like knowing a woman
is driving to my house
with bread to go with my soup.
That we will enjoy a moment
of wild, unprotected
rapport. Then she'll do me the favor
of leaving, allowing me to bend
to where she sat and sniff
the scent of her hair
on the back of a chair. We only
have billions of years to ask
the stars for everything we want.
After that,
there will just be stories of light
people like us have left
for people like them. Whoever
they are. Whatever they wear
or eat. And even if they never bother

to dig up what we have felt
and wanted, it will still be there
in the ground, telling the truth.

Don't say a word

Strange to be alive. I say that
in the conviction I was once a rock.
Living in the mountains
is coming home. Maybe, but the maple
is shaking no. I like the narcissism
of wind better than my own. Do trees dream

of walking away? I'd love to stand
in one place and give oxygen to the sky
to give life to you. If I die today,
this is my last poem. What have I done —
overused *love.* I won't recognize silence,
even when silence is all I've become.

Crossing I Street

This rosebush in Foggy Bottom
has pictures, laminated, tied to it
with string. Of women. Older women.
We've passed it thirty or so times
over the years going to get bagels
or see if the Supreme Court
still smells like mothballs,
a scary fact if you're a fan
of justice, wondering each time
if the women are dead and beloved
by the gardener. It reminds me
of the maple tree I tied
four chairs to when it and I
were kids, they've risen
into the sky for crows
and rain to sit on. I look up
at the chairs and feel clever
yet stupid for depriving them
of a table, as maybe god looks down
and thinks we should have had
three hands and lived twice as long
as we do. Or maybe the pictures
were there first, floating,
a constellation of affection,
and they've grown a rosebush
over time. I don't understand
love or physics well enough
to rule this out, just as it's possible
I once walked away from my shadow.
Yellow roses. Big and fat. Do you think

photos are séances when you look
in the eyes of a dead person
trying to be lovely in that moment
of light? Though it's rude to stare
at the present, it's ruder
not to stare at the past.

The not-so-rough and slightly tumble

We'll kiss and I'll say *I love you*
going to get the mail, then coming back
with a terribly important flyer
for termites or tires, say *I loathe you*
to not boringly reach out for her
in exactly the same way—

a translation she knows to make,
as she knows she can punch me hard
in chest or shoulder and I'll wag
inside and live longer
touching her than if we had never
held hands—

I think it was Baudelaire who wrote,
I love you I love you I hate you
I embrace you I instate you
I predate you I mate you
I conflate you
with everything good, as I should,
if you will bite my forehead,
I will let you in—

or Rimbaud, whose life was sad,
with no chance to wonder
if John Dos Passos ever rode a horse
in the waves off Majorca
and no one like Eve
making spaghetti for dinner
or to think of in a manner

that doesn't feel like thought,
with no carry the one
to it, no what's the deal
with Derrida about it —

and when we walk
as we walk every day,
I find myself saying hello
every few minutes, as apparently
I did as a kid to my parents
each time I ran in or out of the house,
as if I'm not so good
at object permanence or distance,
not so interested in missing a chance
for the jolt of the feeling
of meeting her again
again and again —

by now you're probably wondering
how close I am to perfect —

the only mistake I've ever made
is not thinking of her as naked or me
as equally so beside her every chance
there is —

the chance of now
and now a new now has arrived
to replace the old now
with brand-new shining nowness —

but live and learn —

live and strip and make love
and learn —

live and strip and make love
and get old and learn —

lots to do, lots to do

Looking up is a pain in the neck but I do it anyway

Stargazing's
carbon dating when you're as stuck
on the North Star as I am
in love with the fact
that the identity of the North Star
has changed over the years — as in,
what is fixed
is roving — now Polaris, Thuban once
was more directly overhead —
and Ursa Minor, the Little Bear
the North Star's at the tail
end of, was a dog to the Greeks —
stars and Marlboros
and swallowtail butterflies
and you are all carbon burning
too fast to last much beyond
my noticing a finger snap's
the crumb of eternity I'm given
to adore whatever it is
I'll also overlament
the end of, since I'm essentially
a Romantic Cro-Magnon, a man given
to fits of dumb love — dumb:
speechless, at a loss
for the dross of words —
and better get on with consummating
whatever affairs I care
to have, such as cheating on my wife
with my wife by pretending
to be someone else, a better,

less cynical man — for under
my ardent pretense (see the chuffing
above), it's hard for me
to believe we're much more
than a few elements
briefly sparked to moan
and bark and then go dark
without much loss
to the immensity
that doesn't even see us
taking it all in, which is a cold
fish way to live — but I keep trying
to be enthralled by what goes on
above and around me
enough to help my wife
surmount the doubts we share
that an end awaits
which is spiritually hotter
than entropy, or the cessation
of all that's cool about her eyes
and thighs and thoughts
and that other thing,
the universe

ABOUT THE AUTHOR

This is Bob Hicok's eighth book.

Poetry is vital to language and living. Since 1972, Copper Canyon Press has published extraordinary poetry from around the world to engage the imaginations and intellects of readers, writers, booksellers, librarians, teachers, students, and donors.

WE ARE GRATEFUL FOR THE MAJOR SUPPORT PROVIDED BY:

THE PAUL G. ALLEN
FAMILY FOUNDATION

Anonymous

Donna and Matt Bellew

John Branch

Diana Broze

Janet and Les Cox

Beroz Ferrell & The Point, LLC

Mimi Gardner Gates

Alan Gartenhaus and Rhoady Lee

Linda Gerrard and Walter Parsons

Gull Industries, Inc.
on behalf of William and Ruth True

Mark Hamilton and Suzie Rapp

Carolyn and Robert Hedin

Steven Myron Holl

Lakeside Industries, Inc.
on behalf of Jeanne Marie Lee

TO LEARN MORE ABOUT UNDERWRITING
COPPER CANYON PRESS TITLES,
PLEASE CALL 360-385-4925 EXT. 103

WE ARE GRATEFUL FOR THE MAJOR SUPPORT PROVIDED BY:

Lannan

Maureen Lee and Mark Busto

Brice Marden

Ellie Mathews and Carl Youngmann as The North Press

H. Stewart Parker

Penny and Jerry Peabody

John Phillips and Anne O'Donnell

Joseph C. Roberts

Cynthia Lovelace Sears and Frank Buxton

The Seattle Foundation

Kim and Jeff Seely

David and Catherine Eaton Skinner

Dan Waggoner

C.D. Wright and Forrest Gander

Charles and Barbara Wright

The dedicated interns and faithful volunteers of Copper Canyon Press

The Chinese character for poetry is made up of two parts: "word" and "temple." It also serves as pressmark for Copper Canyon Press.

This book is set in MVB Verdigris, a text face by Mark van Bronkhorst, with display type set in Interstate, designed by Tobias Frere-Jones. Book design by VJB/Scribe.

www.ingramcontent.com/pod-product-compliance
Lightning Source LLC
Jackson TN
JSHW081410170426
101040JS00015B/353

* 9 7 8 1 5 5 6 5 9 4 7 5 5 *